THE DEADWING GENERATION

Simon French

The Deadwing Generation

First published in paperback format by Coverstory books, 2022

This second edition published in paperback format by Coverstory books, 2025

ISBN 978-1-0686701-2-1

Copyright © Simon French 2022

The right of Simon French to be identified as the author of this work has been asserted by him in accordance with the Copyright, Designs and Patents Act 1988.

For details on the cover image - © David Lakin & Tim Shore - see the Acknowledgements section.

All rights reserved.

No part of this publication may be reproduced, circulated, stored in a system from which it can be retrieved, or transmitted in any form without the prior permission in writing of the publisher.

www.coverstorybooks.com

Also by Simon French:

Joyriding Down Utopia Avenue
(Coverstory Books, 2021 & 2025)

Dedicated to the memory of my mum, Shirley French

and to Kayleigh-Anne, Alyssa and Alfie who briefly brought me so much joy before having to fly

Contents

Us	5
The Waiting Time	6
Snow Angel	7
Penny Whistle Hymn	8
Collecting	9
Butterfly Garden	10
New Outfit	11
Wank	12
A Hunter's Moon	13
Buildings You Took Me To	14
King of Chlorine	15
A Walk at Season's End	16
This Photographer Observes	17
Routefinder	18
Birdwatching	19
Flightpaths	20
Kama Sutra for the Canal Age	22
Pedigree	23
Your Last Day on Earth	24
Junk	25
Squeeze Box Buskers	26
Men Who Climb Stairwells	27
Whisky Breath	29
Sleepers	30
Two-Minute Silence	31
Hey Shopper!	32
Kai Tak	33
The Underpass	34
Taken	35
hospice	36
Becoming Alone	37
Caravan	38
Fire	39
Loving the Collector	40
Shoeless	41
Nightlight	42
Spring	43
The Insect Road	44
Roof Space	45
Glider	46

Ballad of Skinny Heart 47
soldier discharged 48
Bottles 49
Coastal Art Hand 51
sons 52
Stylus 53
Anyone Would Have Done What I Did 54
3 a.m. 55
The Cuckoo Spit Messiah 56
Bungalows 57
The Eulogy Bird 58
Hitting the Nail 59
A Diet Comes to Me in the Night-time 60
The Magician is Underway 61
things you need to know 62
Boneyard 63
Ravens 64
A Kingfisher for the Quiet One 65

❊

Acknowledgements 67

Us

We welcome no outsider
until their stomach yelps or their child
bangs louder than a bailiff. Then we're peachy,
then we chip in
with coins from our online pocket.
This is an old country at sleep: also our acne country rising
with Poundland receipts
flapping in hedges like snagged butterflies,
where kids are swatted with Ritalin.
Our knives get restless
without meat. Our rocking horses fall at the last
and every attic insulates itself
with a letter from the front.
We are full of innuendo and wholegrain.
Our most telling memorabilia
is stored in ditches. We suffer chromosome envy,
one-dimensional Empire blues.
Our dissidents walk into lampposts
while we burger ourselves in holy fast-food abandon.
This is my country; a casserole of class aerobics
that doesn't know where its elderly fall.
Yet we know the correct flower
to leave at every murder site,
that body bags in a hangar
will be spaced like the black keys of a piano.
This is our England, cocained, Tudor and flat-packed.
We are a haemorrhage of laughter
but if I'm crying like a standpipe left dripping in the street
then this is my freedom also.
Us Englanders, top-notch at closing curtains
when drunkards are slumped like splitting bin-liners;
happy when our icons deflate onto couches
like parachutes swooning into sea.
We yearn for battlements. Walk the underdog
and with hands shackled
write *sorry* on the back of a matchbox.

The Waiting Time

We apologise that an earthenware sky
floods meagre light into the booking hall.
That no luggage will burst

with anticipation.
You are not permitted to take a turn
around the time zone clocks,

see your face
ticking in each city's distant hubbubs.
Foreign languages

won't be cluttering your ears, your mouth.
Should you decide to sit and wait
we'd like you to be aware

this is not an airport.
No matter that you may wave
your passport or dream of sipping tea

from bone china in Boeing or de Havilland,
our customs and excise officers
have been unavoidably detained. Are unable

to explore you.
If you find yourself believing in arrivals
and departures, we would remind you

that the Ray Ellington Quartet
are providing musical enlightenment
in the control tower.

May we take this opportunity
to disclose to you that starlings circle.
Our propellers are blooded.

We recommend
you leave by the nearest available daylight.
This is not an airport.

Snow Angel

Mum & dad slowly disintegrate
with dividing cells, coronary flutters, tired blood,

watching Panorama, curtains closed
while across the back garden, a dare of virgin snow.

I undress, clothes
collapse to the arctic patio. Penis recoils

like a condemned man
sighting the scaffold.

Scampering to mid-lawn
I lie down in the freezing one-foot powder,

arms flapping like wings & I fly,
carry mum & dad on my back, light as cotton-wools

we tour the night sky.
Next day I spy my indentation. Already the wingspan

shows signs of fatigue. Tufts of grass
pricking the watery membrane.

Penny Whistle Hymn

He drops himself into the ditch.
Sticks a rusty whistle
through the rip in his stitched mouth.

This is the letting go.

Scarecrows walk from far fields,
sit with him to remember his days of menace,
crucifixed among churned clods

when seedlings yelped with life
and birds didn't dare pilfer.
They share a stockpot of turnip, potato

until he's ready to yield his neckerchief
to the snatch of the wind.

Time to drink grog, strong as oxen blood,
from a tin mug said to have contained tears
from the first farmer of soil.

An hour for devotions; they offer
their friend up to the button-eye god
before the unpicking,

the easing of his rope-belt.
Pokes of straw jut from the sleeve
of his dinner jacket and are plucked.

A candle is lit in the unravelment.
They play a hymn on penny whistles
while the fire grows

so hot that crows are forced upward
to scour dust
behind the tractors of a waking moon.

Collecting

I hate myself for taking these photographs
but can't stop. They're not aware.

I'm capturing as many as possible. Slumped
by cash-points. In the doorway

of the shutdown butcher. The smell of piss
marking their territory. I download

the camera's eye into black and white snapshots.
Sleeping bags, cardboard sheets — all the cocoons

pinned to my bedroom wall
and when I sleep, butterflies fill the air.

Butterfly Garden

Butterflies are identified
on the nearby information board
but the airspace is empty.

I'm thinking about scattering her ashes,
not here but down south,
the place she considered home.

Then about going through her stuff,
runs to charity shops,
the local tip.

Best be prepared
now cancer has broken in,
can't be evicted.

I wonder if she's feeling the need
to apologise?
Twenty-seven years ago

I became an aberration of nature,
an abomination
she wished she'd never given birth to.

I'd just come out to her.

Visiting hours loom. I skirt the borders.
Reminds me of Sussex:
hushed in meadow grass,

a young woman and her child
waiting for cabbage whites.

New Outfit

If I was a girl I'd be dopey
as a chrysalis. Let Aaron run his speed
through my open-top hair; 2-seater. Roar
past boys under monkey puzzle trees
and there wouldn't be a crash in the world
to disturb our heartbeat.

We'd be degenerate like clowns
given the chance — mum at the New Baptists,
dad snapping at the aerodrome. Get rumbled
and we'll unzip the coast road;
I'll strum Joni Mitchell from a battered guitar,
a sand song for our frazzled sky.

If I was a woman I'd peel his potatoes
like a bad-assed goddess
bolstered by carnal implication.
Guzzle gin with menace.
Call him a four-inch pilgrim
and hide the shrine.

If I was an old woman
I'd undress on some forgotten country lane,
let rain ping off my xylophone ribs,
play a music from long ago.
Wish me a loud-mouthed sports car
to put the hammer down,

happy to throw myself
into all those dead men's curves.

Wank

My body
stretched into the long grass, skin teased
by shaking blades.

I fell in love with the soil
                                and the danger
that day.

The sun had its grip on me,
seared thoughts of Rob's father
right through me,
                                a slow hawk, high,
my only company.

This was
a switching-on of mechanics,

                                kinetic energy, bristling,

a discovery of all to follow; this pleasure
became an act of giving, the salt winds
full of my dna, chromosomes blinking

in light.

I pulled the life out of myself.

Signed my arrival into the wild world. Fields

different at last.
                                Brushing the sky.

A Hunter's Moon

brightens the old town's face. I smile
   knowing you'll hide in the flagpole's shadow.
We kiss & imagine being lotus blossom
   falling into the quarry's mouth
after the night shift have gone
   to loosen beer
& demand bread from the butcher's wife.

   You wear a shirt patterned with flora & fauna
out of season & your mum hates you.
   We are each other's anarchist. I persuade you
to place cinder on your tongue
   & recite the Lord's Prayer. Your mum hates me.
In a battered Ford
   we aim for roads full of landslide. Return

as boys trapped in a cycle of slate & baptism.
   Hundreds of moons may pass
before we trust the colours of this town's flag,
   before they welcome us to their houses of wet meat
& rusty knives.
   But miracles will happen. You better believe it.

Buildings You Took Me To

Remember you for smuggling me
out of town. Taking me
to buildings with the life sucked out of them

where, like interior designers, we'd position our skin
here or there, kicking away rubble,
the metronomes of sex

disturbing petrol station ghosts.
We walked a silenced railway line. Only one thing
on your mind. Rooting out the ticket office

with sky for ceiling. Once
I saw a daylight moon prying. Good job
it bit its tongue.

You'd have made use of this place. Its ivy rafters.
Its crumbled kilns. Imagine you now
with another young lover

yet to find himself in a building
where emptiness tugs at the sleeve
and unlocked doors refuse to let him go.

King of Chlorine

You were the king of chlorine
but now cramping on the tilebed,
lifted from your rectangled sea,

the lifeguard has flopped you
onto a marble slab, your gills pulsing
as he slits you head to tail,

a filleting knife eases out your backbone,
the stomach opened, scoops of gooey innards
plopped into bucket, pectoral fin

sliced off. You can't believe
this is happening. You'd shown signs
of slowing but surely

deserve respect. You'd outswum the man
doing butterfly, his arms like steel wings
frothing water into cappuccino;

navigated around backstrokers
ploughing into your path.
Even jumpers

didn't dive-bomb as you sharked your way
to the top in the municipal lunchtime session.
Now you're sushi.

Your fish eye sees the lifeguard
survey the fluid ounces of your once kingdom,
keep watch over the up and coming.

A Walk at Season's End

It's a chilly night with keen moon.
Four young men spill from the caravan park,

over dunes. They clutch lager cans.
Peel off shirts, shorts, shoes

and run into the tide. Two girls follow,
herd up the clothing, fold it into piles

and flap a blanket to life. They sit,
chat, laugh, while the men

holler and cuss in cheeky shallows.
The girls struggle with disposable barbecues

but their men have noticed the sea is black
save one trail of moonlight

rippling in its expanse.
They shout their dare to girlfriends,

to shipping lanes, to ghostships,
start to smash the surface with kick and swing.

I walk home, not wanting to know
whether they're still swimming

or perfect tattoos captured by light,
resting in the water's skin.

This Photographer Observes

a thorn bride waiting in the psalmhouse,
cigar-burn in her wedding dress.
Outside, blowtorched air huffs. She barely sips,
smears lipstick on a tin mug
given her by the pastor.
She has decorated the kind of eyes ravens
daren't peck out,
not on a day like this
but her shoulders are wavering;
where is he —
creeping through the cottongrass,
kicking off his shiny shoes?
We have spoken of this before,
his predilection for out-of-town girls,
had hoped he'd find the inner groom
and there's still time.
Her mother and father are also absent
like flags on a windless day
but it's no surprise. This isn't the place
for a man of guns and his vinegar wife.
It's the only photograph I take today.
The moment she lifts off her veil
and opens the window to let the house gasp.
He has finished with her and almost finished her,
her mouth like a split of parched earth, skin
like wattle and daub.
She so wants to fall asleep in the hedgerow,
having gorged from a wicker basket
full of blackberries picked
by other fingers.

Route*finder*

He's taken to wearing a suit
cut from Ordnance Survey prints.

People stare. Some pinpoint & prod
we are here then trace their journey.

He's created a map of his wife,
lavished with grid references. Icons denote

her various stop-off points. A wine glass
for her mouth. A red lightbulb.

When away on business he feeds her
into the satnav

 50 ways to find your lover.

He may have the cartographer gene. It's said
his mother rode the entire Underground

while carrying her unborn.
Either way, when undressing at night,

if his wife confiscates the maps,
he refuses to ask for directions.

Falls into bed.
An empty motorway between them.

Birdwatching

You never see a dead bird
my mother used to say. Not meaning
the idiot-pheasant roadkill or
result of a sparrow
or pigeon's ill-conceived flight plan
via conservatory window.
She meant pensioner bird, stroke bird,
tumour bird that disappears
the minute our backs are turned.

The nurse tells us that often
the dying wait until their loved ones
have left the room
before finally letting go.
Having received the phone call, I return
to find my father cupping her hands,
warming them for me.
I can't cry. She isn't here anymore.

By root of tree,
under fern, in hedgerow. Where the river
curves its spine into the mud bank.
There she is. Learning the language
of dead birds.

Flightpaths

The young man wears black loafers.
Shuffles to the front of the plane. We've taken off
from Croydon. The white cliffs below,
powdered faces, foppish. Dreaming things cliffs dream of.

The young man unwraps a Beretta
from a handkerchief, like it's a holy relic. His face
is pure guerrilla. 47A and 47B
are linking honeymoon arms. This is a highjack.

The young man waves his gun like a baton
and an orchestra of hands raise. He assures us
no-one will be hurt if we don't attempt heroics.
Our air hostess has the look of a battlefield nurse.

47A and 47B put down champagne flutes.
Hold honeymoon whispers.
The young man informs us our skin is soft
as rotting peach. He aims the gun like a hairdryer

at the head in 2C. Mouths dry. His face
is pure Hanoi. Demands the plane divert to Tempelhof.
Our air hostess pours herself into a seat. Below, the Channel
dreams of chasing feet back to shingle.

Among dials and gauges, our pilot sweats. The Riviera
unlikely now. The young man wears slacks. Shirt.
Skinny tie. Gun swings like the hand of an indecisive barometer.
47A and 47B are brushing away confetti.

The young man announces we all have bones
like Capodimonte. His face is pure Suez. Screwed-up
boarding passes hide under seats like dead birds.
Our air hostess comforts the tremble in 2C. Pearls transmute

into rosaries. A honeymoon suite grows impatient.
The young man stands by the cockpit. Has thin-framed
spectacles. Pistol hangs low like landing gear. His face
is pure. States western governments should not interfere

in the affairs of other countries. Emergency vehicles
rush along Alexanderplatz. This is a hijack simulation exercise.
We're complimented on how well we played our roles.
Lessons have been learnt. The skies are safe once again.

Kama Sutra for the Canal Age

Was there ever such a publication? you ask.
We're cramped, floral curtains drawn tight,
not wanting to be a tow-path peep show

for dog walkers, ramblers
and this definitely isn't the time to attempt
our Glowing Juniper or Crouching Tiger.

Hanging tin mugs tattle our lust along the Heron's Rest,

the whispered shushes sluicing from our mouths
as limbs reef-knot together; hips
a steady 4mph and finally water pours in,

lifts us. We're not sure whether lying long-ways or across
was less giveaway
in the delicate art of not making waves.

Pedigree

My ancestors have mouths
like rusty padlocks.
Curiosity buries me in Mercury and Gazette,
hoping for a fluke of reportage.
I hunt for certificates handed out
for exits, entrances, coupling.
A tree grows.
Appears my provenance is rich with turnip pickers.
Farmhands dung-lugging for pittance.
Never slung into workhouse,
no transportation for us.
Modesty prevails regarding wartime bravery.
Seems we've been sportless.
Artless as Rothko.

I descend
from alehouse plotters whose tankard revolutions
sank in the morning slops.
From pedlars of weevil bread, pegs, photocopiers.
I'm not from *slumboy-made-good* dna
or flouncing champagnery (as rumour had it).
There's no trace of puff-pastry faces
or peculiar men spoiling themselves
in the spittle and pox of the highway,
no blaggard seduction from gin palace or chloroform.
Ours is a porridge opera that's built my bone.
For the want of a pile
my inheritance is robbed.
The foxhounds aren't coming home.

Your Last Day on Earth
In memory of Lee Gormley (1982 - 2015)

You were found on a beach towel. Gulls
hadn't investigated. Earlier

you'd walked with shoes held
like hanging fish. Stopped off at a faux-palm bar,

sipped cocktails while its radio frisbeed pop
over sands.

Some girls reported you'd appeared happy,
were amused seeing your bare chest

brag its way into the sea.
It was a pot-roast of an afternoon & later

they claimed, you all chatted
while a breeze frisked you dry.

Even the gods of the riptide
nodded in deference. They considered you

wiser than shark & drowning man. Watched you
fall asleep on your towel.

Hope you like this rewrite. You always
wanted to go to the coast.

A million miles from the bedsit
they found you in. Full of used needles.

Huddled in your duvet.

Junk

I'm crammed with jumble from ex's.
   Fed up storing their deceits,
the arrhythmias dumped at my door.

The showdowns.
   Home truths I've trapped in boxes
with nails always loosening.

The reels of sex
   flickering
as comparison with any new lover.

Want to empty my pockets
   in Earth's orbit.
Let the debris float among space junk

     from jettisons, decommissions,

        the catastrophes

           that created weightless men

               able to leave footprints.

Squeeze Box Buskers

We meet in a closed-down shop's doorway
that could do with perking up.

We sit on rickety stools, an old crate.
Yoska draws the short straw, stands at the back.

I sling an upturned beret to the ground,
it looks like an open mouth, in need of feeding,

then we begin — pulling the air apart,
pushing it back together as songs blow into the street.

Pennies and jeers are flipped our way. We avoid laments
that remind us of the old country,

its leaky roofs,
its wild dogs and our mothers and fathers.

Marko smiles at the pretty girls. His fingers
pulsing out the jaunty drone.

Children stare. Their parents' frown,
weighed down with shopping.

We break for cigarettes and coffee. Today, Pitivo says,
is the anniversary. We shut him up quickly —

don't want him affecting the mood
with his violin or stories of the forest and unmarked graves.

We agree on another Sixties classic, bellow out
its summer tones.

We are here to party. No-one dances
but some feet catch the rhythm.

Men Who Climb Stairwells

just because they're there

are perfectly calibrated
to ascend,
musculature taut & hungry, programmed
for one way;
a lover's apartment,
shoes giving the silence something to think about,
each stair bearing the madness of their rose

or

feet lifting
out of the urination, the clamber away
from a ghostworld of beggars
tracing their outlines
onto concrete,
up past junkies with yesterday's psalms
filleted in pockets;

out to the beauty of municipal neon
& air, to catch constellations
relaxing across the bodywork of cars,
to be as one with the rice bowl food chains
& brazen commerce of the panorama

or

the specially trained officer, adrenalin
looping the loop, pounding, knowing full-well
traffic is screaming below, crowds
barking, *jump   get on with it   c'mon you fucker JUMP!*

   a time to let go
     when the wind has forgotten your name again,
    as your legs dangle like black ribbons
      & an aviary of dead ravens
     has opened in your heart

this stairwell takes forever

or

the gentle tap of a lanyard
against the chest, credit card suit
sharper than a pin in the eye of an angel,
flight after flight, yucca & glass, copper
& beechwood; the blue zone,
Level 9, they come & go;
testing tendon, hamstring,
handrail like the gold line on a target graph,
sweet fiscal dreaming,
breathless,

rest nowhere for too long

in a building that's soldered to the sky,
fills itself with lotus blossom & pictures of old Dresden.

Men who climb stairwells
   just because they're there
should take a photograph of each shoe,
pitch them into a fat wind
& hope they're never invited back down.

Whisky Breath

We're slouched like scatter cushions
on your sofa. Cotton-wool mutterings
tumbleweed from my mouth.
I think about the packed crematorium.
The rise and fall of tissues.
You tell me the dripping tap
in the bathroom is in time
with his favourite song. How you want
to upset a harmonica
and send your blues to the wall.

A clumsy headbutt of a kiss
and guilt gnaws me for taking advantage.
Noosed around your neck
a locket shines, hiding its curls
snipped from Ethan
before the Big C had its way. You melt
like bitumen over my chest.
Awake, asleep,
it's always July. We've both forgotten
to dance or pray.

Sleepers

You peel back the duvet
of a cheap hotel's last bed. Check for stray hairs
like they're insects looking for a new host. Reveal

the mattress and its leaked art. This trampoline of sex.
The cheating husband. An ignored housewife
powered by wine.

You attempt levitation. Want to be as contactless
as a credit card but the bed will not be refused. You fidget.
Imagine the slow-mo waterfalls of drool

that permeated the pillow's geology.
All the kisses that preceded. The plans
and speculations whispered across cotton.

Sleep. The bed has you. Borrows things.
Dreams. Regrets. Hides them to share
with its next guests and by morning has had its fill of you.

You'll shower and restore
to the pristine self. Feel more human
than you ever thought possible.

Two-Minute Silence

A hundred and twenty seconds
of wartime memorabilia
while my head is full of hashtags,
poppered porn, lunchtime menus.
You know what goes on inside of me.
It keeps out the dismantling faces
of this zimmered army with their glitzy medals.
If people around me knew
it could get ugly, the veterans could turn,
their thoughts snatched from billowing generals,
from bone embroidered through Belgian fields.
I'm easily distracted
by the passing stroppiness of call centre girls,
caffeinating businessmen.
I don't know how to find My Deepness.
Wish I could hate myself but you know
I can only hate bacteria, calories, strong sunlight.
I am moisturised.
In my stillness I preen
and you're aware of this.
I catch my reflection in the bugle's sheen.
You don't blow my cover,
let on I have Prosecco in my sights,
that I'm chivvying along the clock and poppy.
I want The Chatter. I want your ear back.

Hey Shopper!

Theft is good soul food.
Leave your carrier bags Unattended
for the whim of thieves.
Let them feast
on designer snakeskin, your dandy electrics,
the Swarovski hoard.
Consider now
Un
encumbered/Undistracted.
The mind freed. Un

leashed.
After all
Newton's apple wasn't Faberge.
Imagine a liberation from key/insurance.
Door & window, Unclenched.
Remember this;
Einstein's equations
were not his safe combination.
For pity's sake — only if you're robbed blind
can you hope to be returned.

Kai Tak

Good business opportunity you said.
Did your best to persuade.
Teased me with the daring of Kai Tak's runway
fingered into Kowloon Bay. I stuck
to England.
Soon you had skyscrapers growing
from the limited plots of your skin. *Gweilo*
they called you. This was your Hong Kong,
monkey-brain air and monumental acts
of commerce. Intoxication
with this Jenga isle that never topples, that offered
24/7 silk boys, hoopoes on the nightwire
and lobbies haunted by air-con.
Where you fell for dried seafood,
could re-enact the ocean in your belly.
And all the time your feet grew
as light and sleek as hotel elevators
taking you to a place of wanton enlightenment.
You were never coming home. I learnt
the true weight of gravity by being grounded.
Often wonder when it was
I ran out of runway.

The Underpass

        is assured of its own temptation
understands the tricks it can play   on your mind
makes you think   you'll see the light   any minute

escape its failed neon   on route to
the rest of your life   on foot or behind wheel
you pass stockpiles of litter   feel

you've cheated the gridlock   with no price
to pay   you may be cautious   scurrying through
a single female   with pepper-spray bravado

knowing a little more footfall sees you emerge
a radiant homo sapien   into the bars & casinos
of the plaza   soon forgetting its lichen   dripping water

the feel of a pilgrim's way
welcoming hybrids   charabancs   Deliveroo riders
chasing their business   yet its designer remains

shadowy   its walls sneer with hieroglyph & anarchy
it will not prevent the stoned driver
introducing himself at 60mph   or

knife angel muggers idling for a victim   your booty
exchanging hands   it only desires
a chalk outline for your body   will instruct the wind

to race its length   raise you as dust   so make peace
with concrete   don't voice disdain my friend
the echo always finds you

Taken

I worry that a fundamentalist
might snatch my favourite gnome.
Place him at the foot of some monument.
Teach him fist-pumped songs.

Worse still, an extremist
bundles him into the back of a van.
A social media release threatening
to chainsaw through red collar, beard.

I'd fret. Wait for the ransom note. Imagine
him gagged, watching his captor
polish a gun with spittle & pride.
There'd be no Stockholm Syndrome. My gnome

wouldn't want anything to do
with the old women of sectarians
in headscarves & buckled shoes
lining the route of a march. Can picture

rosy cheeks puff as he hears sacred words
leave the megaphone. Caught on CCTV.
Rod held firm. Hook dangling
in air full of fish.

hospice

mother lugged her carcass over the world's final wall

in an act of stillness   and agony   only partially muffled by morphine

she did it from the mechanical bed   with nurses in full bloom

wrapped in sky   offering placebo smiles

   I'd wanted to take her pain   but she insisted I was too sentimental

told me she was harbouring a ball of growing meat

in her belly   and how wonderful that death

comes from life comes from death   celebrate

don't waste your time believing in ghosts   she whispered

I've met them   they're not worth the salt and the dust

and I have no sorrys   the braille of scars I etched into you

will make sense

will keep your blood fuming   and sharp

   I wanted to return the warmth she'd lent me as a slippery baby

plucked from the tub   her body deepening into its own cold

a gradual decommissioning

her one scrap of strength saved for the heaving   over the wall

she warned me

the only door is stubborn oak   the key always lost

Becoming Alone

Dad mopes in the hollow house. Half-dusts.
Pinches laundry onto the washing line.
Rounds up apples as she would have.

At evening he slumps in the lounge.
Remembers air heaving with garlic, thyme,
her condensations

haunting the kitchen window.
When she was inundated by steam,
the shower's perspex, moistured

like a rainy day; the waft of botanicals.
Says he feels apparitions of her breath
settling like dew on his neck.

Dad wishes he were like a dehumidifier —

her wet inside him

drawn down past circuitry,
pooling in a sacred lake
for the moonless animals that gather to drink.

Caravan

hogs the drive. Nomad at rest.
Pastiche of hotel. Fat box.
Its four travelled wheels

under mud pack. Single. Towbar
reaching out. Tickled by privet.
Itching for road.

Getaway. A touch of cosy.
Children lark across the leatherette.
Contrast with the plain veneer

of motel or B & B
with carpet overworked.
Walls pitted.

Glowing dinette,
a battleground for whist. A prelude
to the world beyond dralon.

The full-stop odyssey. Trapped
by rain. Percussion
of moody Dorset. Father

drains the Elsan Blue. Escapes tempers
that flap like caged birds.
Berth of the blues.

Stodgy traffic. Summer
breaks. Job done. Feel for the caravan.
Tethered again wanderer.

Fire

You brought us unimagined warmth, roasted our arrow kill
into the earliest carvery. The cave as ideal home.

Trapped you behind glass, hoisted high on coasts & estuaries,
let you jitterbug for boats to pinpoint anchorage.

In your debt for turning the heat up under cedar,
sandalwood, myrrh. Evicting them from the hang & swing

of iron burner, to create perfume
from holy elsewheres that rules the air.

You perk things up in the seducer's bedroom.
Place you on candles in a chorus line of light,

you offer ignition for the post-coital spliff, the passing
of the Olympic flame. The basking.

Happy to do the dirty stuff. You hunger for sticky swabs,
excavated tumour, dispatched

in the terrible smoke. Are always patient
as we wring out goodbyes before you launch our dead

into a stained-glass sky.
We are the perfect partnership. Can have fun with you.

Juggle you. Jump through hoops of you but most of all we ask
you turn your back on arsonists, anarchists, the torturers

who'd cage a man wet with petrol.
Let their caves be damp, bones brimming with frost.

Sit them around our spent campfires. Have them warm their hands
over ash.

Loving the Collector

You relax
in one of your 1930's chairs. Online bidding
has turned your skin to Bakelite, your eyes
into art-deco portholes. You feed me
gramophone jazz in the hope I won't ask
the price of your latest find. I fidget.
Prefer comfort over style. You say you'll make
a modernist of me yet. Quote Josef Frank

> *I like the overall effect from a distance better
> than the individual motifs*

I know where I sit.
I am chrome. I am catalogued.

Shoeless

Never needed the rucksack sun.

I'm without horsewhip or arrow's intent. My gaze

on calm fish. Grass stretching. Paints drying.

Far from boredom's ache. But

thank you for mechanicals that rushed me

into transport networks. You,

a man of nuts & bolts, whose spiritual elevation

came from the incantations of Trivago or satnav.

You told me it's a white-knuckle world, to keep

breaking borders. I was always drawn

to the ignored silences. Lost. Mulling.

Our love is now exhaust fume,

an old warmth in the ozone.

You'll hail your next hectic tuk-tuk. Gust

past shrines. Eat from a street vendor whose fan

struggles with your heat

while I'm barefoot again, idle as a baked river.

Letting the breeze carve its patterns into me.

Nightlight

Swirled with thousands
around the ashing of a portly bonfire.

Plucked you from your buggy,
Saturday 3rd November 2007 at 6.30pm.

You were busy being five months old.
In my arms, can't quite remember how

I angled you
so you could see fireworks burst

in the toffee-apple air. Covered your ears.
Didn't want exploding decibels

to damage your hearing.
Your mum and dad laughed.

Arms ached for days after
but it was a good pain.

Three years on
you'd been adopted, so won't have been told

about Saturday 3rd November 2007 at 6.30pm,
your mum and dad, me,

you lifted in arms to face a sky
that's already forgotten the hullaballoo,

being covered in reds and purples
like glittering bruises.

Spring

detonates the garden

feel the feather of wind

on your neck   convince yourself

you are a part   of the whole

that life   is good

but   will you ever

make an entrance   like the wasp

attempting breaststroke   across scrumpy

or move an audience

like a field mouse   in owl shadow

you have a gut feeling

that whatever variation   the year whistles

you have more in common

with the back legs   of the centipede

disappearing

under weights of stone

The Insect Road

We stop running. Spit out aphids. No idea why

but you want to shock suburbia. So two boys kiss. I get
a lungful of you. Longer than expected. Nine seconds.

Dirty bastards   You need exterminating
I decide gardeners
are control freaks with watering cans & infestation.

We walk out on the posh houses.

The park once won an award.
It has an ornamental bridge & when you force one hand
down my shorts, the other over my mouth

I don't pull your hand away
as my mouth is full of words that have lost meaning.

Then we do butane & figure Jesus underachieved.

Consider cooling our feet in the brook.
Dogs are barking at the end of every distance. Maybe
we'll have dogs one day.

Right now I want us to be filthy again
in some shady motel room of undergrowth
so dark we can't hang our shadows

to frighten birds but hey!
we can leave our shapes in the soil. That's a start.

Roof Space

My friend's life shrunk to OO gauge.

Lockdown, with underlying health issues

& a crazy virus

conducting house-to-house searches.

In his attic, he expands

a small world of track, train, into a resin town

in a rush to go nowhere.

With time on his fingers

the slim controller is God

but even gods have to sit in waiting rooms

on occasion, watching the commute

of a centimetred people. Delay. Derailment.

Glider

hauled off land by a Cessna
umbilical cord cut

the wind's mouth shouts
like English Punk

we navigate humps & divots of air
i tense

can see horses like beads of oil
sliding around Goodwood

& a barcode of ploughed land
scanned by sun

the pilot asks
if i want to take control

just want to land
not be suspended

in this escalating sky
where every ambition

has forgotten its parachute
where i have no choice

but to ride out the thermals
wonder what the ground

has in store for me

Ballad of Skinny Heart

Skinny Heart
suffers its first breakage.
Why has she left it? Something it said?
Is there another it?
Skinny Heart
punches its world of bedroom,
scatterguns the garden in angst rap.
It heads out
full of sour leanings
to where barley fields tilt and whisper
and it first cozied-up to her.
Where exhausted lager cans
got ditched into plough tracks
after she and it
drowned each other's mouths
and clothes scattered.
It frets — a bag of sobs
dousing dry earth.
It will return home,
follow the scuffmarks
of all previous *its*,
learn how to shuffle
the maidens of the estate
with its thrusting gab,
its crock of fidgeting hormone.
Skinny Heart, eatless, sleepless,
unaware it's building scarecrows
to be poked
into the churned-up soil.

soldier discharged

you dive for cover
into shop doorways
under duvet

the perimeter
of your exit wounds
wet with vinegar

your father taught you
to be tough as steel

but now you are helpless
an anonymous streak of meat

the moon plucks the string
of your sleeping body

but no sound plays
to the hardening night

it's as if you're sealed up
have roadblocks inside

there's nothing more to do
than shake the sand
from your boots

let us fill our mouths
with the desert
you find endless

Bottles

The alcoholics are polite today, bottles tidied away

at the back of their cupboards

or chilling in the cistern; an old trick that still delivers

but it's not always this way. Sometimes

they stumble into mischievous furniture.

Keel over like circus clowns without the happy paintwork.

Then the side us poets like, & social workers call chaotic.

Where demons shout like they're on a talk show.

Where demons harangue like they're at a demonstration.

The dark has so much promise, he used to say. He would.

He couldn't change a lightbulb

so became bat-like in his quest to find the drinks cabinet.

Yes, the alcoholics are polite today. Ordered.

I have nothing to write home about. Take Shyona.

She's been picking blackcurrants & now she's making jam.

Not a jot of liquor sipped for years.

Social workers & poets are not needed. The vulture in me

will never swoop onto Shyona's corpse, tug chunks of meat off. She is

a living meringue who'll die a meringue. Nothing to sustain me there.

Pisshead is not a term of endearment. It should be

& it should be remembered that echolocation is not infallible.

He tripped on the kerb before ever reaching Oddbins.

Lay on the pavement, mouth open,

drinking rain like it was the most beautiful gin from Heaven.

Coastal Art Hand

positions himself on a rousing shore,
hoping dog walkers or beachcombers
don't poke their curiosity into his oils.

Already the gulls annoy him
like popcorn chatterers in the back row.
He's fascinated by fits and starts of climate,

the way they influence the ocean.
He'd like to capture something
of this maritime bile rolling in,

is feeling pressure — doesn't want rain
to streak his colours
or light to lower itself any further

into the waves.
He notices his latest blotch of cloud
has a look of his wife's face,

anaesthetised onto canvas.
He decides on a suitable hanging.

sons

sons of miners
                dig holes for themselves
in parks behind boarded-up working men's clubs
their lungs filling with cannabis

sons of shipbuilders
                    stand in puddles
on streets behind empty pubs and corner shops
hands working the ring-pulls of easy booze

sons of trawlermen
                  scatter their weight
along some rocky curve   night-fishing
torchlight skimming pools where sealife is trapped

and feet
        illuminated against the milk stout black
walk on estuary water   over ferry lanes
fall through ocean holes   maybe they hope to find wrecks

that once bore their fathers' hard-fought nettings
grab corroding metal
                  never let go

Stylus

In a beginning, boy-men of the 70's,
grounded at desks. Heads full of vinyl song.
Pocket-money flexing to buy guitars, drums

and all the time the Universe encroaching.
We were in a different gravity
from would-be mechanics, soldiers, dentists

who sneaked off behind bike sheds
to experience solar winds fanning smoke
from a B & H

or feel the big bang theory
turning pages of Penthouse or Mayfair.
Just passing time in class

with A4 planes launched
behind the teacher's back.
We were going to sell zillions.

Good then we passed on
to our children
the folds and flaps,

those flimsy dimensions of a paper plane
that might one day
just dare to loop the moon.

Anyone Would Have Done What I Did

I imagine walking into the train station.
I'm aware of a terrorist
primed with nails, dynamite
or whatever Acme bomb-making equipment
he's strapped into. Would I jump him,
smother the blast, mop up the ballistics
like a sheet of kitchen roll? The unsuspecting
fuss over arrivals/departures. Are they worth
my life? My future beer and anonymous sex traded
for the legal secretary, the banker, dozy students.
Imagine my legs flustering like a palsy.
I'm no wrestler, writhing on the platform
with some half-cocked martyr. Would end badly
for me. This is no ordinary day.
You can't possibly be prepared
for partisan pronouncements slung through a crowd.

Or would the wimp in me run?
Genes more selfish than they've a right to be.
Sweating out into beautiful acres of pavement,
traffic — the promised land. Ducking
to avoid the livid eviction tearing through air.

I practise the line for reporters. For family.
I'm minutes away from the station. Fuss
over my departure.

3 a.m.

my father informs, is not the time to stir.
He swears he's woken by insistent eels,

thwarted by the industry of beavers.
He's now a river that punches like a brook

while the moon swells like a frog's vocal sac
and the dripping tap taunts.

He remembers his drinking days,
brags ten pints a night

was once possible, when his bladder tensed
full of bravado, tough as the Krays

and sleep was nailed to the bed frame.
3 a.m. is just the start. My father warns

of the balloon inside, taut
as a trumpeter's cheek, the last piss

before the dying of the bathroom light,
except it's not. Leak. Stain. Clench.

I'll celebrate at the urinals of Costa, of motorway
services, when the ghosts of coffee leave

without a fight. My father reckons
this alone is our greatest achievement.

The Cuckoo Spit Messiah

'Religion will eventually become as offensive and unacceptable as racism.' - Chris O'Dowd

Bump into the Cuckoo Spit Messiah,
he's adjacent to my early morning radio song,

tells me over toast he is wise enough to be
on first name terms with the moon. Impressive.

We sip espresso. He senses
my prior griefs. Calls them ballast for the soul.

Hang on to his every word. Expect oral goo
but he keeps me waiting. Points out blemishes;

an absinthe here, an amateur porn flick there.
I am uneven at my door & should leave tofu offerings

for the wild furs of night. His mouth still not
expelling slobber. Take a shower. He insists on watching.

You don't refuse the Cuckoo Spit Messiah.
Lather my chest, penis & balls

with fake botanicals. He announces the spirit
is trying to enter me. I explain innuendo.

Consent. Pain.

He licks his lips. They remain arid as lizard skin.
Hands me my towel & is gone.

On the kitchen diner a note — *you are the remnant
of your prayers, indecisions & petty exuberances*

& your espresso is cheap. Whatever.
Some radio song becomes a ghost. I switch off.

Bungalows

can nod off. Are retiring. Favour
garden cities or seaside towns.
Vote in elections. We suspect
they tell everyone

the year they were built. Like to keep
a tidy garden and defy hosepipe bans.
They have no natural predators
although are wary

of developers. Their attics
are congested and places of melancholy.
Some spend afternoons
watching tv quiz shows. It reminds them

of imparting knowledge.
We believe they evolved
from elders' mud huts, revered
and turned to by all in the village. Now

the upstart Barratts and Wimpeys
think they know it all. The mock-Tudors
look down on them. They keep quiet. Wait
for the day we ease onto their doorsteps.

The Eulogy Bird

sits in your tree, is prepared
to be patient, still believes in your promise
although rather disappointed
to find you pottering in the greenhouse
with a frown hovering above every flaccid snapdragon,
every suicidal marigold.
Aphids fly rings around you
and you being you
decide it's best to break for tea.

The eulogy bird trails you at a discreet distance,
makes excuses for you
still has hopes you'll squeeze out that novel,
just one best seller, the one you've had
knocking about in your head since you were a young man
impressing girls
with the rattle of words.

Right now the eulogy bird could call it a day.
Fly off. Find some more deserving person.
But the thing about these birds is they don't give up.
Once one gets you in its sights
it's with you for life.

You sit in the garden, mulling over
whether your knee would hold out
if you entered the charity fun-run;
musing over whether you shouldn't have shouted
at the young mum who cut you up in the supermarket aisle
with her disabled son's wheelchair
(yes the eulogy bird saw
but chose to turn a blind eye),
or whether you should switch on your laptop
and click on the file *Chapter 1*.

The eulogy bird is giddy in anticipation
and in equal measure worried,
knowing how hard it is
to create plausible fiction.

Hitting the Nail

you're as useless as an indoor parachute
my partner taunts, then jumps from the sofa.
I dream of being handy. Using the hammer
like a magician's wand. He's planning
to heal the injured wall. Descending.
Eighteen inches to go. The world in slow-mo.
Truth is my fingers have always been
unfamiliar dance partners. My father
was ashamed at my lack of DIY skill.
Tried to pass on knowledge
but only spoke to my headless body. Didn't
notice my head had left the room, doing things
like reading, eyeing up
the boy next door. Attempting to be
the next Lennon or Bowie.
Twelve inches from ground. I think
can I do something to impress? Fix the fence to thwart
the tiptoe of wildlife & the criminal fraternity?
Rewire a plug? Outsmart voltage
& avoid the great shock?
He's five inches from laminate floor.
Spread your arms I shout, *make like wings!*
We prepare for impact.
I have whisky waiting. It's good
for softening the blow.

A Diet Comes to Me in the Night-Time

I'm not full of famines so I throw sugar over my shoulder.

Watch the face sink with celery. Wasting. Oh such hollow miseries,

but I'm not a child deep in Africa's unbalances. Even so,

no other species check their waistline. Count calories

in the kill before them. My stomach throws its cutlery in protest.

I've been hiding foie gras in the medicine cabinet. Loaves of bread

disguised as miracles hang from the ceiling. Temptation

for the eye's rupture. I cheat

in *B.O.G.O.F.* nirvana. Remind myself supermarkets are not consecrated

though they wear the robes. Get back to the hallelujah treadmill,

the millponds of sweat beneath me. Am I disordered? Is anorexia

a core aesthetic of diet or just walking backwards in the hall of mirrors?

Hell, the whippets are on the catwalk.

This will do me no favour. Want to stuff my compulsion

in a brown paper bag. Let it seethe among fly-tippings.

The topography of my body transforms. No mammal can locate

the place of prayer & longing. Their tongues like wet crispbread,

lick me all over in salty bewilderment. I am lost & wasted. Nature

headbutts a vacuum

& my entirety is held together by a belt chasing its own tail.

The Magician is Underway

Children sit cross-legged on the parquet,
party hats skid off heads
bobbing with intrigue.

Parents shuffle uneasily
at the back of the community hall
as The Great Encora cracks open the ribcage

of the shy boy dragged to the stage. *Bloodless illusion*
the showman yells as a sparrow flutters
from the chest cavity, aims for rafters.

Next he scoops out Phoebe's eyeball. *Ergh*
go the children, then gasp
as from the socket he produces a toffee

no-one wants to eat. With gusto
he gags and binds Olivia,
promises wizardry that can only happen

in a tall Oriental cabinet, forces the birthday girl inside,
utters the spell that transforms her
into the woman she will become, naked

as the day her mother pulled her from a pocket,
she steps out to applause, cord and gag
falling. Her voice will be free.

things you need to know

i slept with a man who believed only water tells the truth.

he lived in a chapel & was full of nettle stew & guilt.

every week someone would leave a loudhailer

on his doorstep not knowing if he had wisdom to spare.

the ghost of a moth he killed last year circled us at night.

he drove an old army jeep. late summer

gave him the dust to hide behind. you know him.

he has a photograph of you. taken

when you could charm kites on a windless day.

it's nailed to a telegraph pole & the poacher

wants to stuff it in his howling pocket. today

our differences are on display. my stomach raw & holy.

you picking chickweed & listening

for capsized mouths singing from the river.

we should leave them to their autopsies. collect our footsteps

in a paper bag. scatter them along the road.

let's leak our autographs onto the estuary's lips.

i'll become water tugging you down.

you will be the lie that keeps us afloat.

Boneyard

They have come from the sky
like dead servicemen repatriated.

You see thousands of Boeings, Airbuses
held in a suspension of desert,

their vital organs removed,
sent to recipients around the world.

Tired metal plays a slow Morse code
with the sun.

Two workers in shades
are extracting seats

with dental precision,
a row of four conjoined,

placed in the Arizona sand
like an outdoor cinema.

Reminds you of buckling up
with your family for the last holiday

you were to spend together.
You watch as fuselage is blowtorched,

sparks pour themselves
into the shape of electric flowers.

Already the wind has begun ushering
dunes across your shoes.

You thread your fingers
through the perimeter fence.

It's time for the sky to be simple.

Ravens

It is said the kingdom and the Tower of London will fall if the ravens ever leave the fortress.

Ravens tense on my shoulders.
Our nostalgia is contagion laced with liver-spot bunting.
Feel like deconstructing with squalid fecklessness.
This is maypole in flames. Death shops with its loyalty card.
Look for speeding hearse. Headless driver.
I am still here.

We are a sweepstake.
Took England to the races. She wore bandage
and safety-pin, a golden fascinator. Lost her fortune
to the fat bookie in a merciless hat. We can't feel joy.
Guests moor their Mediterranean dinghy

in our water feature. Weep. Yet it only takes an analgesic
and we become kind as tin.
Continue living in the angry haphazards of town
to plug the exit-wounds of bus shelters, fox fur, squaddies.
We are still here.

You are a utility. An under-valued commodity
seen walking down Railway Terrace, raw folk
practicing the algorithms of poverty. Later you may feast
on wild mushrooms and charity syllabub. Celebrity chefs goad you.
Your voice inconspicuous as a drug mule. No-one wants to hear anyway

but if you're lucky you'll karaoke in a ghost bar. Part-smoked Rizlas
flutter at your feet like moths past caring. This is your watershed.
Do you know what's turning in the cauldron? Your gravity knives
will become birds of prey.
You are still here.

This is my ambiguous country,
stitching itself up as fast as we unpick it. Guernica
is my screensaver. I am blemished by this pantomime of politik.
The jester mocks each virtue, vice, lamentation
that has soiled its way out of me. Ravens leave my shoulders.
I am a vacancy.

A Kingfisher for the Quiet One

There are plenty of rivers to sit on the banks of.

Fat rivers full of contraption and remnant,
cocky rivers juggling fish, or rivers
catwalking with blossom and Kodak promise.

In my grief

I feel guilt that I can't quite remember
the curves of your voice,
your blush, those blue gin eyes. The edges of you

smudged.

So I've been drawn to our river,

attempt to reinstate you, working back
to before you became the ash we draped
on the hill's wind

and this is the sorcery of rivers
because try as I might

you refuse to join me
but on the backs of minnow my wishes ride

and during sleep the river breaks in, courses
through my bedroom. You glide above its surface.
Take human form in your cyan dress. Talk

about farmhouse Julys. Dad's train collection.
The letter from your consultant.

Then you leave.

Look! I am your son woken. Perched in light.
Wingless. I lean into the colossal air. You are
everywhere.

Acknowledgements

Front cover artwork by Tim Shore.
Back cover photo by David Lakin.

Previous publications:
- 'Butterfly Garden' first appeared in *Dream Catcher* (Issue 33, June 2016)
- 'This Photographer Observes' - 3rd Place in the Kent & Sussex Open Poetry Competition, 2018 (Judge: Helen Ivory)
- 'The Waiting Time' - 2nd Place in the Kent & Sussex Open Poetry Competition, 2019 (Judge: Ruth O'Callaghan)
- 'sons' first appeared in *Prole* (Issue 28, April 2019)
- '3 a.m.' - shortlisted for the Bridport Poetry Prize, 2019 (Judge: Hollie McNish)
- 'Boneyard' - highly commended in the Winchester Poetry Prize, 2019 (Judge: Helen Mort)
- 'Fire' first appeared in *Ink, Sweat & Tears* (Online, November 2019)
- 'Bungalows' first appeared in *Snakeskin* (Online Issue 269, February 2020)
- 'Kama Sutra for the Canal Age' first appeared in *Prole* (Issue 31, May 2020)
- 'Your Last Day on Earth' first appeared in *Snakeskin* (Online issue 272, May 2020)
- 'Pedigree' was commended in the Winchester Poetry Prize, 2020 (Judge: Andrew McMillan)
- 'Coastal Art Hand' first appeared in *Orbis* (No. 197, Autumn 2021)
- 'Becoming Alone' first appeared in *Lighthouse* (Issue 23, January 2022)
- 'things you need to know' first appeared in *The Interpreter's House* (Issue 77, April 2022)

Many thanks to Derby City Poets and the Derby Stanza for their invaluable advice and support.

www.ingramcontent.com/pod-product-compliance
Lightning Source LLC
Chambersburg PA
CBHW051552010526
44118CB00022B/2682